Remembering
Anaheim

Stephen J. Faessel

TURNER
PUBLISHING COMPANY

This aerial view of Anaheim was snapped on July 14, 1953, and begins to show the growth of the community outward from its downtown core. By now many of the area's orange groves were being paved over for housing—the city's population had surpassed 22,000, an increase of more than 7,000 in just two years. By 1955, Anaheim would embark on a journey that would make it the entertainment and tourism destination for Southern California.

Remembering
Anaheim

Turner Publishing Company
www.turnerpublishing.com

Remembering Anaheim

Library of Congress Control Number: 2010923499

ISBN: 978-1-59652-629-7

Printed in the United States of America

ISBN: 978-1-68336-803-8 (pbk.)

Contents

Reinforcing Anaheim's position as an international destination, on December 21, 1976, Anaheim signed its first "Sister City" agreement with Mito, Japan. We see Anaheim Mayor Bill Thom and Mayor Pro Tem John Seymour join Yunosuke Wada the Mayor of Mito, and Kan Kimura, Chairman of the City Council of Mito, in ratifying the official declaration. The Sister City program gives communities of different nations a forum to share ideas and information. In 1998, Anaheim's second Sister City became Victoria-Gasteiz, of Spain.

ACKNOWLEDGMENTS

This volume, *Remembering Anaheim,* is the result of the cooperation and efforts of many individuals, organizations, and corporations. It is with great thanks that we acknowledge, in particular, the valuable contribution of the Anaheim Public Library for their generous support.

We would also like to thank Stephen J. Faessel, our writer, for valuable contributions and assistance in making this work possible.

————————

As the author, I would like to thank Ms. Jane Newell, Local History Curator of the Elizabeth J. Schultz History Room, Anaheim Public Library, for her very generous assistance and support in the creation of this book. Mrs. Ymelda Ventura and Mr. Sal Addotta, History Room staff, have also contributed their time and encouragement to this project. Thanks to a special friend, Marcie, for enlightened guidance.

Finally, I must acknowledge the loving assistance of my wife, Susan, for her unwavering support of this undertaking. Without her it would not have been completed.

PREFACE

Anaheim has thousands of historic photographs that reside in archives, both locally and nationally. This book began with the observation that, while those photographs are of great interest to many, they are not easily accessible. During a time when Anaheim is looking ahead and evaluating its future course, many people are asking, How do we treat the past? These decisions affect every aspect of the city—architecture, public spaces, commerce, infrastructure—and these, in turn, affect the way that people live their lives. This book seeks to provide easy access to a valuable, objective look into the history of Anaheim.

The power of photographs is that they are less subjective than words in their treatment of history. Although the photographer can make subjective decisions regarding subject matter and how to capture and present it, photographs seldom interpret the past to the extent textual histories can. For this reason, photography is uniquely positioned to offer an original, untainted look at the past, allowing the viewer to learn for himself what the world was like a century or more ago.

This project represents countless hours of review and research. The researchers and writer have reviewed thousands of photographs in numerous archives. We greatly appreciate the generous assistance of the individuals and organizations listed in the acknowledgments of this work, without whom this project could not have been completed.

The goal in publishing this work is to provide broader access to this set of extraordinary photographs that seek to inspire, provide perspective, and evoke insight that might assist people who are responsible for determining Anaheim's future. In addition, the book seeks to preserve the past with adequate respect and reverence.

With the exception of touching up imperfections that have accrued with the passage of time and cropping where necessary, no changes have been made. The focus and clarity of many images are limited to the technology and the ability of the photographer at the time they were recorded.

The work is divided into eras. Beginning with some of the earliest known photographs of Anaheim, the first section features images from the earliest period, 1865 through 1899, with a focus on Anaheim's vineyards. The second section spans the years 1900 to 1939, taking a look at the city's citrus industry. Section Three moves from 1940 and the World War II era to 1953. The last section covers the years 1954, with the advent of Disneyland, forward to recent times.

In each of these sections we have made an effort to capture various aspects of life through our selection of photographs. People, commerce, transportation, infrastructure, religious institutions, and educational institutions have been included to provide a broad perspective.

We encourage readers to reflect as they go walking in Anaheim, strolling through the city, or wandering its parks and neighborhoods. It is the publisher's hope that in utilizing this work, longtime residents will learn something new and that new residents will gain a perspective on where Anaheim has been, so that each can contribute to its future.

—Todd Bottorff, Publisher

This 1858 view shows August Langenberger's two-story adobe store and residence. In 1857, Langenberger, the son-in-law of Juan Pacifico Ontiveros, partnered with another Anaheim pioneer, Benjamin Dreyfus, to start the town's first general store. The Langenberger's home was on the second floor and an adjoining large room was used for dances and other social functions. Ruggedly built, the adobe survived the historic flood of 1862 and was finally razed in 1915 to make way for a business block of modern buildings.

THE MOTHER COLONY

(1865–1899)

Anaheim's second mayor, Henry Kroeger, built the Anaheim Hotel at the southwest corner of Lemon and Center (now Lincoln Ave.) streets in 1871. Advertised with "well lighted and heated" rooms, the interior furnishings were of high quality. Max Nebelung was the proprietor for many years. Renamed the Commercial Hotel in 1890, it passed through a number of hands before being sold to John B. Ziegler in 1905, who operated it until 1915 when it was razed and replaced with the Hotel Valencia.

This view of Center Street (now Lincoln Ave.) from around 1873 faces west past Los Angeles Street (now Anahcim Blvd.). Paving would not come for more than 40 years. The rural character of the town can be clearly seen. Anaheim's impressive, although financially fragile, two-story Planters Hotel is visible at center. This structure replaced the original Planters Hotel that burned in 1871, but it too burned on the morning of July 5, 1890. The hostelry was never rebuilt, the vacant lot taking the name Planters Park.

A local dog relaxes in the afternoon sun in this view facing east on Center Street (now Lincoln Ave.) from Lemon Street. The Anaheim Hotel, later named the Commercial Hotel, is visible at right. Center Street remained the main commercial thoroughfare in Anaheim well into the late twentieth century.

Anaheim's 1884 Fourth of July parade makes its way down Center Street. The horse-drawn wagon is driven by Nick A. Bittner, foreman of Anaheim's Volunteer Confidence Fire Company #1. The volunteers were organized in October 1883 and took every opportunity to participate in local events. Their bunting-draped wagon also sports a pump organ.

From the tower of Central School, Anaheim's two-story Planters Hotel is visible at the corner of Center Street and Los Angeles Street. The Planters Hotel, built by Anaheim pioneer and first postmaster John Fischer in 1865, burned to the ground in 1871; the second also was lost to fire, in 1890.

The Los Angeles stage has just arrived at Anaheim's Planters Hotel here in 1882. When rebuilt after the first structure burned in 1871, local advertisements noted that it was "Lighted With Gas" and that "no pains or expense has been spared to make this in every respect a FIRST CLASS HOUSE!" Despite the hyperbole, the Planters never lived up to the financial expectations of its various owners.

Bavarian-born Benjamin Dreyfus's first winery on Center Street is shown here in 1884. In 1857, Dreyfus formed a partnership with August Langenberger to run a mercantile store in the new town. Standing third from the right of the wine barrel, Dreyfus organized the Anaheim Wine Growers Association, which acted as a marketing agency for member vintners. His firm, B. Dreyfus and Company, had become California's largest wine distributor by the late 1870s.

Around 1885, Henry Oelkers plows the William Koenig vineyard on South Los Angeles Street (now Anaheim Blvd.). Oelkers came to Anaheim in 1884 from his native Hamburg in order to assist his uncle, William Koenig, in his winery.

Doctor James Hovey Bullard and two friends stand in front of his office on Los Angeles Street (now Anaheim Blvd.) in 1885. In addition to being one of Anaheim's pioneer physicians, Bullard also ran a modest winery.

In 1885 Dr. James H. Bullard bottles a recent pressing of local grapes. Winemaking was often a small affair with the vintner doing a great deal of the work. Bullard also purchased a stock interest in the Anaheim Improvement Company, which planned to build the much-anticipated Del Campo Hotel.

These substantial, brick business buildings indicate the success that the original colonists had in creating a growing community from the dry scrub of the Santa Ana plains. This view faces west on Center Street (now Lincoln Ave.) from the corner of Los Angeles Street (now Anaheim Blvd.). Within the next few years, the crop on which this economy depended would be lost and the colonists would eventually find a profitable substitute.

The Fritz Ruhmann building at 217 North Los Angeles Street in 1886. Ruhmann, a native of Schleswig-Holstein, arrived in California after being shanghaied at Hoboken, New Jersey, in 1875. When his sailing vessel dropped anchor at Anaheim Landing several months later, Fritz was given his freedom and met Max Nebelung, who introduced him to a number of his fellow countrymen living in Anaheim.

From around 1886, this view of the Joseph Backs store at 125 North Los Angeles Street shows Joseph Backs at far right and Joseph Backs, Jr., at center. In addition to maintaining a thriving mercantile store, Backs also served as the town's undertaker.

West Center Street in 1887. Lafayette Lewis started the Fashion Stables, on the south side of the street, in 1872. The Commercial Hotel with its signature balcony is visible on the corner of Lemon and Center streets.

The region experienced a land boom in the 1880s and both real and paper communities were platted. Seen here is the Hudson Real Estate office advertising building lots for a modest $100. Among those pictured are Dr. A. V. Fox (3rd from left), Dr. V. C. Hardin (4th from right), Adolph and Frederick Rimpau, D. W. Hudson, Fred Smithe, Joseph Helmsen, and William Harker.

Lafayette Lewis arrived from his native New York in 1872 and opened the Fashion Stables on Center Street. Anaheim's streetcar line was incorporated by Anaheim's first mayor, Max Von Strobel, but his death in 1873 stalled construction until 1887. The one-mile line connected the Southern Pacific Depot on the west side of town to the Santa Fe Depot on the east side. It never generated the income foreseen by its owners and quietly closed in 1899.

This 1888 view of North Los Angeles Street (now Anaheim Blvd.) shows the Palace Market owned by Mr. D. A. Brunswicker, and F. & J. Backs Furniture and Undertakers. Anaheim's downtown streets sported coal oil streetlamps, permitting some evening shopping.

The Goodman and Rimpau Building, the Langenberger Building, and Anaheim's Planters Hotel can be seen in this 1888 photo of Center Street facing west from the corner of Los Angeles Street. Many of the wooden buildings of earlier years were beginning to be replaced with substantial brick structures, indicating the financial success of the original pioneers.

The Anaheim vintners established a port south of Alamitos Bay originally called Bolsa Chiquita. In 1857, just after Anaheim's founding, Frederick Schneider established the Anaheim Lighter Company to ferry goods from the anchored ships to the shore. This area became known as Anaheim Landing and was popular as a seaside vacation destination in the last years of the nineteenth century.

Anaheim Landing, despite its treacherous ocean outlet, enjoyed popularity as a vacation spot for the whole of the Santa Ana Valley. A number of semi-permanent tents were erected for the convenience of visitors.

Once regular railroad transportation became available in Anaheim after 1875, Anaheim Landing became more of a seaside attraction than an active port. This 1891 portrait features a vacationing family enjoying one of the vacation cottages that were available. Today, as part of Seal Beach, this area is known as Anaheim Bay and rests inside the U.S. Navy Naval Weapons Station.

Here in October 1891, the firm of Wille and Albrecht installs a new 60,000-gallon water tank at the town's municipal water works plant at 119 West Cypress Street. Anaheim's frugal German trustees started their city-owned water department in 1879 to generate a small income for the community. The original facility had one shallow steam-driven pump and a 20,000-gallon redwood tank, which served most of the domestic water needs of the town's 883 residents.

This 1891 elevated view of Anaheim faces west down Center Street from Los Angeles Street. The two-story brick Backs building stands to the right of center. At this time, Anaheim had not moved far beyond its original boundaries of North, South, East, and West streets.

The stagecoach was still an important mode of transportation prior to the twentieth century. Anaheim was a popular stop on the stage route between Los Angeles and San Diego, as much for its saloons as for its bustling business district; the German settlers maintained a "wet" town for the convenience of citizens and visitors.

For the Fourth of July, 1892, celebration, Anaheim erected a double triumphal arch. The city built a number of arches in the early years to recognize the nation's independence. Although usually substantial edifices, they remained standing only through the celebration and parade.

A rabbit hunting party stands in front of Frank Ey's barbershop in 1893. The men and boys proudly display their catch and possible dinner. The "country" was just outside town and hunting was an activity widely pursued.

Pictured here is the ornate building of the Citizens Bank of Anaheim.

Kistler's Boston Bakery stood at the corner of Los Angeles Street and Cypress Street from 1891 to 1896. Identified from left to right are Stephen Kistler, Miss Mary Kaiser (Stephen's sister-in-law), and Caroline Kaiser Kistler (Kistler's wife). In addition to baked goods, the Kistlers maintained an ice cream parlor, much to the delight of the local youngsters.

Mable Street in West Anaheim was home to the Evergreen Nursery, owned by Timothy Carroll, an Irishman who arrived in Anaheim in 1863. His well-respected nursery supplied most of Anaheim's early agricultural rootstock. West Anaheim School (later renamed Loara School) and the Hund residence are just visible in the background.

Around 1894, the newly constructed Metz Block building occupies the southeast corner of Center Street and Los Angeles Street. Built by Margaretha Metz in memory of her late husband, John, who died in 1869, this impressive structure dominated downtown Anaheim for many decades. Isaac Lyon's hardware store occupied most of the first floor.

By 1895, William Boyd had taken over the hardware business located in the Metz Block. Boyd supplied the growing community with housekeeping necessities including "Quick Meal Gasoline Stoves." The Cowan dentist office and the Pacific Boarding House occupied the upper floors.

A late 1890s view of Center Street facing west features various buildings on both sides of the street flanking the Anaheim Streetcar tracks. Identified left to right are the Palace Restaurant, the landmark Metz Block building, Bentz & Steadman Meats, S. S. Federman clothing store, the telegraph office, post office, and Pellegrins Music Store.

In 1894, the entrepreneurial city trustees entertained the idea of electrifying the community. When a Los Angeles firm offered to install and operate streetlights in the downtown area for $125 a month, Trustee Joseph Helmsen claimed that the city "could easily maintain the plant on their own account." A $7,000 bond issue followed for construction of the "500-light" plant located on West Cypress Street. On April 11, 1895, Charles Lorenz, the town's oldest living resident, "pushed the button" inaugurating Southern California's first municipally owned electric utility.

Electric streetlights have arrived in downtown Anaheim in this late-nineteenth-century view east on Center Street (now Lincoln Ave.). Fred Pressel's Blacksmith Shop at 218 West Center stands at right. The tracks of Orange County's second oldest horsecar would be removed in 1901.

The stately Del Campo Hotel was located at the northeast corner of Broadway and South Olive streets. Erected over a period of two years (1888–1890), it was built and furnished with quality materials. Despite its impressive reputation, financial setbacks forced its closure and conversion into the Pacific Sanitarium and School of Osteopathy in 1896. In 1905 the hotel was sold and razed, the resulting serviceable lumber sold for $6,000, and the lumber used to build a number of houses.

The Knights of Pythias, Anaheim Lodge No. 105, parade down Center Street in the late 1890s. The Knights of Pythias was founded in 1864 as an international, social brotherhood that promotes the principles of friendship, charity, and benevolence.

E. H. Susmil stands in the doorway of his harness shop in the 100 block of Center Street (now Lincoln Ave.). Susmil occupied the ground floor of the two-story Kroeger building, built by Anaheim's second mayor, Henry Kroeger.

Anaheim barber Willard A. Frantz and postman Frank Eastman, advertised as having "the first trained Ostrich in the United States," trained ostriches in the early years. Their two running stars were named Napoleon and Josephine. The two men and one of their stars pose for the camera at the Coronado Beach racetrack in 1896.

Frank Eastman, Anaheim's earliest mail carrier, appears here in his R.F.D. (Rural Free Delivery) horse-drawn mail carriage. Anaheim's R.F.D. Route 1 covered most of the town of Anaheim in 1896, when this photograph was made. Eastman covered the route on foot before building his homemade carriage.

In view here is the front of Anaheim's Del Campo Hotel. A group of Anaheim locals enjoys the hotel's expansive porch. Although an impressive building and lavishly furnished, the hotel was not a financial success and was converted into the Pacific Sanitarium and School of Osteopathy in 1896. Its brief career ended in 1905 when the property was sold and the building razed.

A late-nineteenth-century interior view of Richard Henry Seale's neatly arranged grocery store. Bert F. Fulwider stands in front of the left side counter; Seale stands at right. By this time, many of Anaheim's business houses were sporting electric lights, which arrived in 1895. This improvement, long awaited by the local businessmen, permitted evening shopping.

Ten local business leaders of the Anaheim Ways and Means Committee pose outside Cornelius Bruce's Candy Kitchen at 106 East Center Street (now Lincoln Ave.) ca. 1898. Identified left to right are Louis E. Miller, E. P. Fowler, W. J. Newberry, Capt. Irwin Barr, John B. Rae, E. B. Merritt, Henry Kroeger, Cornelius Bruce, August Nagel, and J. P. Zeyn. Bruce, in addition to his candy store, maintained the town's lending library in the rear of his building.

Federman & Co. was one of Anaheim's premier clothing merchants in the last days of the nineteenth century. Their store, housed in the Federman Block building, was located at 102-104 North Los Angeles Street (now Anaheim Blvd.). This substantial brick turreted building was an Anaheim landmark for many years.

A group portrait of the children from Anaheim's Central School, recorded in the waning years of the nineteenth century. The school, at 231 East Chartres Street, was built in 1877 and housed elementary through high school grades. This edifice held the distinction of being the first school in California built through the sale of bonds.

Charles E. Bauer maintained a blacksmith shop in Anaheim at the turn of the century. The blacksmith, in addition to his regular duties as farrier, was also the town's general repairman and mechanic. Activity in Anaheim was enough to keep Bauer and his competitor Fred Pressel quite busy.

August Langenberger's Wells Fargo and Co. Express building was built in 1875 at the corner of Center Street (now Lincoln Ave.) and Lemon Street. For many years it housed the Dickel Grocery and Hardware Store, with the local telephone office upstairs. This landmark structure survived until August 1925, when it was razed for the construction of the new S.Q.R. department store. The horse-drawn vehicles on the street demonstrate the continuing importance of horsepower in turn-of-the-century Anaheim.

The residents of St. Catherine's Orphanage have their portrait taken on March 21, 1899. In 1887, the Dominican Sisters arrived at the urging of the pastor of Anaheim's St. Boniface Church, Peter Stoetters, to start a new Catholic school. Unable financially to survive with the twenty students who attended, the sisters turned the school into an orphanage. Later, with a fall in the number of orphans, the sisters converted the facility into a military school for boys, where it continues today as St. Catherine's Military Academy.

The photographer opened his lens from the top of the Del Campo Hotel to expose this view of turn-of-the century Anaheim. To the south is the residence of Mr. and Mrs. C. E. Ramella, at lower left, and the home of George E. Boyd, co-owner of the Orange County Preserving Company, at lower right. Anaheim's rural character is conspicuous, with houses still having the required "outbuildings" as well as the windmills that pumped water.

The new century had just dawned when this photograph of Fred Pressel's blacksmith shop was made. Located at 218 West Center Street (now Lincoln Ave.), this was the first of two that he built at this address. The Pressel family continued their business presence in Anaheim well into the late twentieth century.

Citriculture Brings Growth

(1900–1939)

The Peerless Bar, owned by Andrew Fuhrberg, was one of several drinking establishments in the town. Anaheim at one time boasted more saloons than churches, a fact that the residents of many "dry towns" in Orange County appreciated. In this 1903 view, Oscar Renner, one of the three owners of Anaheim's S.Q.R. mercantile store, stands at far right.

Anaheim had long been a baseball town with a number of fraternal and business organizations fielding teams. Shown here is the Anaheim Baseball Team in 1900, with the young players identified left to right: (back row) Edgar J. Hartung, Bill Fischer, Theodore Dickel, Elmer Stone, H. Westerman, and Fred Conrad; (front row) Ned Merritt, Charles H. Fischer, Lafayette A. Lewis, and Dwight Stone.

Rudolph "Rudy" Fossek was employed by the city to sprinkle the town's dusty streets from 1902 until 1913. Here in 1902 Rudy and his new 700-gallon horse-drawn wagon work the streets of early Anaheim. Fossek also joined the town's volunteer firemen at local fires to provide an additional water supply. In 1913, business interests finally persuaded the frugal trustees to begin paving the important streets of town, rendering Rudy's task obsolete.

The Commercial Hotel is draped in patriotic bunting on July 4, 1903. Built by Anaheim's second mayor, Henry Kroeger, the Commercial Hotel was located on West Center Street at Lemon Street, and was one of Anaheim's popular hotels until replaced by the Hotel Valencia in 1916.

This 1904 image shows Anaheim's own Company E of the State Militia, posed at attention on the steps of the Del Campo Hotel. Most towns maintained militias, which were more often called for parade duty than to protect the residents.

C. G. McKinley ran his feed yard and ice depot at 111-113 North Los Angeles Street. In addition to wood, coal, hay, and feed, he was the town's exclusive supplier of Aetna Mineral Water.

The second railroad to reach Anaheim was the Santa Fe, which entered Anaheim in 1888, building this wood frame depot at 708 East Center Street. The arrival of the Santa Fe provided competition to the Southern Pacific, which had reached Anaheim in 1875. A rate war ensued that ignited a regional real estate boom complete with speculators, brass bands, paper cities, and free lunches for potential landowners. A group of travelers poses for the photographer at the depot in 1905.

Anaheim's Philadelphia Street is lined with neatly maintained homes in this 1907 view. Right to left are the residences of Sidney and Emma Holman, Cornelius and Zilphia Bruce, Ira and Hilda Chandler, George and Ina May Dietrich, and Thomas and Ellen Hollingworth.

John Wirsching sits in his mule-drawn wagon in front of the Anaheim Union Water Company building at 123 North Los Angeles Street here around 1905. Wirsching's wagon was a rolling billboard for his "Advertising Agency."

Charles Fischer ran Chilie's Place, a pool and billiards hall, located at 112 North Los Angeles Street. A place for men to relax, these establishments, filled with tobacco smoke and spittoons, were shunned by the town's proper ladies.

Anaheim's growth exceeded the capacity of its original electric and water works on West Cypress Street at the turn of the century. On April 14, 1906, Anaheim voters agreed to indebt themselves in the amount of $46,000 for a new utility facility. A lot was purchased on South Los Angeles Street and after many debates, the new facility was finally erected. Anaheim's new very-modern powerhouse went "on-line" December 20, 1907.

Around 1908 on Broadway at Los Angeles Street stand the large home of Dr. Herbert A. Johnston on the southeast corner and the home of Dr. William Wickett, just behind. In addition to being neighbors, both doctors were partners in the Anaheim Sanitarium, later named the Johnston-Wickett Clinic.

Shown here in the early twentieth century is Napoleon Hart's Place, located at 117 East Center Street. Dee Jackson stands behind the ornate bar, and Anaheim's Duke Paschall stands on the left. Hart's Place kept an interesting stock of spirits, wines, and cigars for patrons.

The Anaheim Knights of Pythias Lodge No. 105 chartered this Santa Fe train on February 13, 1910. The special train brought 1,500 brother Knights members from Los Angeles to Anaheim for an initiation of 118 new members into the Anaheim Lodge. A local Knight is seen greeting the train while riding a goat.

The interior of the Exchange Bar, located at 132 West Center Street, in 1908. Identified left to right are Sam Morningstar at the bar, William F. Stark, proprietor and mayor of Anaheim from 1920 to 1923, and A. L. Walter behind the bar. Anaheim's early German heritage ensured that wine and spirits were never far from hand. The coming of Prohibition in 1920 would close this interesting chapter of Anaheim businesses for many years.

By all accounts, Anaheim's favorite saloon was Roman Wisser's "Favorite Saloon" located on West Center Street. Lucien "Pete" Wisser, Roman's son, ran the business after Roman's death. The advent of Prohibition in 1920 forced the family to establish a new business. Wisser's Sporting Goods became an Anaheim landmark, supplying the town's children with their first bicycle, pocketknife, or baseball mitt.

Buster Brown Shoes holds a promotion day at the William Falkenstein Store ca. 1910. Falkenstein's, located at 101 West Center Street, was for many years considered the town's premier department store where the town's businessmen would buy their Florsheim shoes, Hart Schaffner and Marx suits, and Arrow dress shirts.

Broadway School was built in 1908 at the corner of East Broadway and South Olive streets. The building was enlarged in 1914 to accommodate kindergarten and additional students. The stately building appears here around 1910 as originally constructed.

On February 5, 1911, Anaheim's first El Camino Real bell was blessed and dedicated in front of the Adelheid Steam Mineral & Electric Bath Parlor at 212 South Los Angeles Street. These bells were installed throughout California to signify the route of the Padres as they established the early Mission system in the Spanish-controlled California of the late 1700s. The El Camino Real (Kings Highway) passed through Anaheim from San Diego to Los Angeles. Mrs. Adelheid Koenig sponsored the bell to commemorate this early trail.

The interior of Richard Fischle's Mission Ice Cream Parlor in 1911. Located at 124 East Center Street, it was a very popular stop for the young and old alike in early Anaheim. A public-spirited person, Fischle served as the city's fire chief in 1924.

On April 6, 1911, the local Knights of Pythias marched in funeral procession down a drizzly West Center Street for their beloved member, Herman Kruger. Pallbearers included Herman A. Dickel, John W. Duckworth, Henry M. Adams, Clemens Amberg, John Hahn, and N. J. Kuhlman. Kruger was the promoter and builder of the Anaheim Sugar Factory, one of the town's early industrial firms.

Visitors to the 1911 Anaheim Carnival are preparing to ascend in the Balloon Ride. Once airborne, they will see the roughly one-square-mile town surrounded by walnut and Valencia orange tree groves.

In 1911, the Anaheim Carnival ran from September 29 through October 1 and attracted visitors countywide. Anaheim, as the oldest and one of the larger towns in the county, was already known for its many forms of entertainment. For those who could manage the 10-cent admission, food booths, a balloon ride, and a sideshow featuring "Dirty Dora" were offered.

Anaheim's 1912 Fourth of July celebration included both automobile and motorcycle races in addition to the usual parades. Alfred "Butch" Bittner won his "Fine Silver Loving Cup" for completing the 20-mile motorcycle race in 24 minutes, 6 seconds. Butch is standing behind his winning 7-HP, 2-cylinder Indian Twin motorcycle.

Anaheim's frugal trustees began to pave the city's streets by the mid teens, finally realizing a long-held dream of the street-side merchants. In this 1914 photograph Anaheim's city fathers are showing off the city's new Elgin Motor Sweeper in front of City Hall. From left to right are Bill Sackett, Mayor John Cook, Councilman John Brunsworth, and Charles Mann. Bud Sackett, Street Superintendent, is at the controls and Bill Stark is sitting forward.

With the advent of paved streets, the pollution emitted by horse-powered transport was ever the more conspicuous. Fritz Stolt, here at work on East Center Street ca. 1914, was employed by the City of Anaheim to keep the thoroughfares free of the hazard.

Morris Wampler Martenet, Sr., started his hardware store in downtown Anaheim in 1910. This 1915 view shows the interior of the store at 125 West Center Street. Martenet poses in the background at right, behind a row of wood-burning stoves. His store was known as the place to buy the heavy stoves and other hardware needs the growing town required. Martenet's son Morris "Morrie" Martenet, Jr., later inherited the business and served as a city councilman from 1932 through 1942.

Anaheim's Salem Evangelical Church was located at 400-402 West Center Street in 1915. This impressive brick and stucco structure served the congregation into the mid twentieth century.

After Anaheim lost its grape industry in the late 1880s to blight, the propagation of the Valencia orange became the town's most important concern. The Anaheim chamber of commerce took every opportunity to promote Anaheim as the "Capital of the Valencia Orange Empire." In this 1915 view, two boosters are promoting "Anaheim California, Home of the Finest Sunkist Valencia Oranges."

The 1915 Anaheim Central School faculty has boarded a truck for a picnic, presumably to Orange County Park (now Irvine Park), a regular destination for such relaxing events.

Joseph Backs is seen in the doorway of his upholstery shop at 112 West Chartres in this view from around 1915. Joseph's brother Frederick was the town's undertaker.

The Ingram Brothers Ford Motor Cars Garage and Sales Room was located at 228 North Los Angeles Street (now Anaheim Blvd.) in 1916. A variety of models are advertised from $665 to $765. By this time, the horse and buggy was losing out, although citizens of lesser means would keep their stables for some years to come.

At the Anaheim Steam Laundry employees pose for the camera on a portrait day in 1917. Located at 412 South Lemon Street, the two-story building was a landmark for many years. It was sold to the Theodore Brothers in 1918, who constructed a new building, which later burned.

During World War I, the patriotic citizens of Anaheim contributed $425,000 to the fourth Liberty Bond Drive, $100,000 more than the goal. This four-sided sign was placed at Anaheim's main intersection of Center and Los Angeles streets.

Lee's Service Station at 604 East Center Street was the first individually owned service station in Anaheim. Built and operated by Lee Geiselman, it featured Ventura Gasoline. Here in 1920 (left to right) are Ralph Maynard, Harold Ritchie, and the proprietor, Lee Geiselman.

The May 30, early 1920s, Memorial Day parade float features a Salvation Army hut in the Argonne Forest. A number of Anaheim boys had seen service overseas in "the War to End All Wars," and this float was very meaningful.

The Gerrard Brothers & Hanson Grocery Store was located at 249 East Center Street at North Emily Street. This store opened in 1923, before the partnership was incorporated as Alpha Beta Markets. Lars Hanson was manager of the chain's Anaheim store No. 12.

Excavation for the basement of the new Angelina Hotel is under way in 1923. Completed in 1924, the Angelina was one of Anaheim's better hostelries. Alex's Tamale Factory and the Anaheim Union Water Company offices are visible along Philadelphia Street in the background.

The three-story American Savings Bank Building (formerly the First National Bank Building) was located at the Southeast corner of Center Street and Los Angeles Street. Conspicuous in this image from ca. 1923 is Anaheim's landmark flagpole, in the middle of the intersection.

Anaheim's 1923 California Valencia Orange Show had by this time found a permanent home at the future site of Anaheim's La Palma Park. This year's theme was "Egyptian Settings" attributable in part to the recent discovery of King Tut's tomb and the high interest it had created.

The interior of the 1923 California Valencia Orange Show offers a glimpse of the Egyptian theme for this year's event. The large tent included all kinds of displays, each centered on the Valencia orange, the region's most important agricultural product. Contests were held at these events and prizes were given for the best exhibit, as well as to the local orange packinghouse with the fastest packer.

In 1925, this "permanent" Moorish arch entrance to the California Valencia Orange Show was built, featuring an 85-foot tower that contained a searchlight. The French Renaissance was this year's theme, and exhibits filled a 200-foot by 400-foot tent. The shows held four exhibits: Citrus, Automotive, Industrial, and Amusement.

A parade through downtown Anaheim opened the 1928 California Valencia Orange Show. The theme was Aladdin's Lamp and the Anaheim float was decorated accordingly. More than 85,000 visitors attended the event, which filled a tent covering 400,000 square feet—reportedly, the largest tent ever erected in the country.

Anaheim's Boston Bakery had moved into more substantial quarters by 1924. Located at 201 East Center Street, the popular store would soon be razed for the construction of Samuel Kraemer's new American Savings Bank of Anaheim.

In 1890, Anaheim's early brick mason contractor, Charles Schindler, built this imposing house at 422 West Center Street. By 1928, the home had been converted to the "Orange County School of Fine Arts" depicted here. The Queen Anne Victorian structure suffered extensive damage in the March 10, 1933, Long Beach earthquake and was the first building scheduled for demolition.

Warren Hodges at left and Frank Dotts are shown standing in their garage business at 306 North Los Angeles Street in the 1920s. The partners had a reputation with fast cars, much to the dismay of the Anaheim police force.

Picking time at Theodore Rimpau's orange grove, at 309 South Palm Street (now Harbor Blvd.). In 1962, this became the site for Anaheim's new central library. In this view are (left to right) George Wells, Wells's son, Frank Jennings, Wells's younger son, Frank Clark (on ladder), Archie Cadman, George McAuley, William T. Wallop, and Billie Cooper.

Baseball greats Walter "Big Train" Johnson (pitcher for the Washington Senators) and Babe Ruth of the New York Yankees, played an exhibition game at the Brea Bowl on October 31, 1924. The teams were playing a benefit game for the Anaheim Elks Christmas Charity Fund. Later in the evening, both players served as grand marshals of Anaheim's inaugural Halloween parade.

Seven friends are driving their 1917 Jordan Touring car around Anaheim streets, advertising the 1924 silent movie *Sea Hawk* previewing at the California Theater that evening.

The Anaheim city band is playing in the street at the corner of North Emily and East Center Street in the 1920s. Anaheim had several community bands over the years that were popular for many occasions and celebrations, from hotel openings to Fourth of July parades. Anaheim's 1913 Masonic Lodge building is visible in the background.

In 1925, the streets of downtown Anaheim are sporting new five-globed ornamental streetlights, concrete sidewalks, and paving, much to the relief of the street-side merchants. Automobiles have now completely replaced the horse and mule as the preferred mode of transportation, and brick and tile buildings have replaced the lightly built downtown of years past.

The Bethel Baptist Church at the corner of South Broadway at Lemon Street was dedicated in 1927. It replaced the original 1903 German Baptist wood-framed church built on this site.

Anaheim's American Legion "40 & 8" Post members march alongside their horse-drawn float in a 1920s Armistice Day parade.

In 1857, George Hansen, the surveyor who laid out the town of Anaheim for the Los Angeles Vineyard Society, built this pioneer home, the first "modern" home in what would later become Orange County. On March 14, 1929, the "Mother Colony House," as it became known, was dedicated as the county's first museum. Donated to the city of Anaheim in 1954 by the Daughters of the American Revolution, the house remains today a beloved tie to the community's past.

After many years of debate and two unsuccessful trips to the polls, the community finally voted
in 1920 the $100,000 of bonds required to purchase land for the city's new public park. Another
$100,000 park construction bond followed two years later, resulting in Anaheim's new moniker the
"City with the Beautiful Park." This major civic improvement included goldfish-filled lagoons, a
lighted softball diamond, picnic grounds, tennis courts, an Olympic-sized pool, and an amphitheater
that could seat 2,000. This was a remarkable commitment to local recreation by a community that
numbered less than 6,000 residents.

The Hotel Valencia, at the corner of Lemon Street and West Center Street, was built in 1916 by John B. Ziegler. It occupied the same corner where both the original Anaheim Hotel and the Commercial Hotel had stood. Designed by Anaheim architect M. Eugene Durfee and costing a formidable $40,000 to build, it was one of Anaheim's premier hotels for many years. This mid 1930s image shows both the First National Bank and the Oyster Loaf Café as first-floor tenants.

After a number of years of discussion, negotiating, and political wrangling, ground was finally broken for Anaheim's new post office on May 29, 1936. Eventually built for $86,000 and located at 121 West Broadway, this federal station continued to serve the postal needs of the community until its demolition in 1996. Here the officers of Anaheim's Masonic Lodge #207 officiate at the ceremony.

Around 1936, the chamber of commerce's latest publicity idea was to send one of the area's famous Valencia orange trees directly to New York City. This image of the truck and its precious cargo was recorded outside Anaheim's 1923 city hall building. Mayor Charles Mann (in the dark suit at doorway of the truck) is surrounded by local residents, who are wishing the truck and its important cargo good luck.

After several days of heavy rain, on the morning of March 3, 1938, the Santa Ana River broke through its banks and flooded most of northern Orange County. Anaheim was especially hard hit owing to its proximity to the river. This view captured the morning of the flood shows South Los Angeles Street from Broadway. In the background is the municipal water tower adjacent the powerhouse, where operator Oren Morey sounded the first warning whistle at 4:15 A.M., waking Anaheim's sleepy residents to the impending disaster.

This view of North Los Angeles Street later the morning of the flood shows the receding floodwaters. Once the water drained away, storekeepers needed to deal with flooded basements and ruined merchandise. The basement of the telephone building on North Lemon was inundated, cutting off all phone service in the stricken community.

Anaheim's new La Palma Park featured a full-size hardball diamond and concrete bleachers. The chamber of commerce strongly promoted the facility, which, together with the area's mild winter climate persuaded Connie Mack's Philadelphia Athletics to make Anaheim their spring training grounds from 1940 to 1942. An exhibition game held in 1940 shows Anaheim police chief James Bouldin trying his luck in the batter's box.

A City Is Born

(1940–1953)

Orange County production of the Valencia orange peaked in 1938 when more than 9.3 million boxes, worth $16.9 million, were shipped from local packinghouses. Anaheim's Mediterranean-like climate, dubbed the "frostless belt" by local boosters, was ideal for the propagation of this kind of citrus and was home to a number of citrus packers. The interior of Orange Belt Fruit Distributors at 805 East Center Street is pictured here in 1940. Local women worked seasonally and handled the actual grading and packing of the fruit. Pictured from left to right are Marcella Gomez, Chonita Veyna, and two unidentified women packing Orange Belt's Three Star brand.

The Henry Brothers Drug Store is visible in this April 1946 view facing north on Lemon Street from Center Street. The upper floors of a number of downtown business buildings held apartments. The Roberts Apartments were located above the Henry Brothers store.

Facing east on Center Street across Lemon Street in April 1946. On the south (right) side of the street are the S.Q.R. department store at 202 West Center, the Southern County Bank at 184 West Center, the Hotel Valencia at 182 West Center, the Oyster Loaf Café at 174 West Center, and Rommel's Café at 170 West Center.

Comedian Jack Benny was the nation's most popular radio personality when on January 7, 1945, he included the name of the town in his famous "train leaving on track 5 for Anaheim, Azusa, and Cucamonga" comedy skit. Anaheim's chamber of commerce wasted no time proceeding to "adopt" Jack as their own native son. Plans were finally made to have Benny visit Anaheim during its Civic Progress Week celebration on April 21, 1947. The star arrived at the Anaheim Elks Clubhouse in a 1906 Maxwell driven by local Judge Raymond Thompson and surrounded by most of the community. Six-year-old David Faessel was surprised to see the famous radio voice in person.

Anaheim's annual Halloween parade is marching west on Center Street here in 1947. The small float and costumed children illustrate the Hansel and Gretel story. By this time, Anaheim's old California Theater had been converted to a Fox Theater and featured a new, modern lighted marquee. The double feature today includes both Rex Harrison and Maureen O'Hara.

Anaheim's population was nearing 14,000 by 1948 and Center Street was its main thoroughfare. The county's tallest structure, the six-story Kraemer Building, is visible in this image of East Center Street. The F. W. Woolworth Store is also visible at 115 West Center as well as the Bank of America at 201 East Center Street. Urban redevelopment of the early 1980s would demolish all of these business buildings except the Kraemer, the last reminder of Anaheim's bustling post World War II downtown.

Anaheim's bustling downtown with its many shoppers in 1951. The 1950 census had just counted 14,522 noses, and records show that by this year the population ticked closer to 16,000. To the right is the S. H. Kress five-and-dime at 218 West Center Street, their large candy counter a favorite stop for parents with children in tow.

WHERE THE WORLD COMES TO PLAY

(1954–1960s)

In August 1954, the McNeil Construction Company is preparing the grading for Disneyland. In just 11 months, Walt Disney's dream of a new kind of amusement park, for children and adults alike, would open in this dusty field, now devoid of the oranges and walnuts it produced for the old Anaheim families that had owned the land. Once the new "park" opened on July 17, 1955, Anaheim, and Orange County, would be forever changed.

This north-facing aerial view of Disneyland recorded on June 7, 1958, shows the park surrounded by Walt's favorite attraction, his narrow-gauge steam railroad. The area around Disneyland retains the agricultural flavor of the region, now fast disappearing with the construction of motels, shops, and other tourist-oriented businesses. West Street is on the left side of Disneyland with the new Santa Ana Freeway, Interstate 5, running diagonally across the top.

In view here in the 1960s are two of Disneyland's favorite early attractions. The Submarine Voyage opened June 6, 1959, featuring eight 52-foot submarines that took the visitor on a journey through "liquid space." The Monorail ride opened June 14, 1959, as the Disneyland-Alweg Monorail System, Alweg a Swiss firm that contributed to the design. When in 1961, the ride carried visitors to the Disneyland Hotel across West Street, it was the first time a monorail had crossed a public street in this country.

Anaheim's Halloween parade was begun in 1924 and by the 1950s was a leading civic event. The 1957 parade included a float from the S.Q.R. department store that featured three women dressed as witches in a haunted forest. By this time, the parade was beginning at La Palma Park, whence it proceeded down Los Angeles Street (now Anaheim Blvd.) to the downtown area.

In order to meet the library needs of Anaheim's expanding community, a "Bookmobile" service was inaugurated in 1958. Making a regular route through the outlying parts of the city, it was a welcome addition to the city's literacy program.

Anaheim's police department introduces its new roof-mounted-speedometer police car at La Palma Park in 1959. Designed to patrol the community, it reminded the residents to "Check Your Speed."

South Los Angeles Street (now Anaheim Blvd.) ca. 1960. In this view north from Broadway Street, Anaheim Pickwick Hotel at 225 South Los Angeles Street is visible at left. Built as the El Torre Hotel by the Pickwick Stage Lines in 1926, it served as the firm's bus station and also housed a number of small businesses. It served the community in a variety of roles until its demolition in 1988.

Dubbed the "Big A" for its landmark scoreboard, Anaheim Stadium appears soon after its completion in this aerial view. Costing $15.8 million and seating 43,204, the facility was formally dedicated on April 9, 1966, with an exhibition game with the San Francisco Giants that drew 40,735 fans.

The Anaheim Amigos were one of the Anaheim Convention Center Arena's first tenants. The Amigos, a team of the newly created American Basketball Association (ABA), played but one season in Anaheim before leaving for the Los Angeles Sports Arena. Unable to secure a national television contract, the ABA dissolved in 1967.

The 1968 Mobil Economy Run, a 41-car competition, left Anaheim for Times Square, New York, on Sunday, April 7. One of the drivers was sixty-six-year-old Gertrude Blair DeWitt, who had driven taxicabs in New York City for 38 years. Her passenger was Anaheim City Councilman Orda L. "Chuck" Chandler, who planned on boosting Orange County's tourist attractions on the 3,000-mile course. "Anna," Anaheim's 600-pound elephant mascot who had earlier "washed" Ms. DeWitt's taxi, poses for the camera.

Notes on the Photographs

These notes, listed by page number, attempt to include all aspects known of the photographs. Each of the photographs is identified by the page number, a title or description, photographer and collection, archive, and call or box number when applicable. Although every attempt was made to collect all data, in some cases complete data may have been unavailable due to the age and condition of some of the photographs and records.

Printed in the USA
CPSIA information can be obtained
at www.ICGtesting.com
JSHW072023140824
68134JS00042B/3753